A Thin

Pink

Ribbon

Teri Carlson

ISBN 978-1-63885-052-6 (Paperback)
ISBN 978-1-63885-053-3 (Digital)

Covenant Books, Inc.
11661 Hwy 707
Murrells Inlet, SC 29576
www.covenantbooks.com

For everyone fighting breast cancer, those who have survived it, and especially those who have lost their battle with this disease.

I also give appreciation and love to mother, Patricia Hagerty Brennan, whose life was cut short by breast cancer after a brave fight not once but twice. It was her memory and strength that saw me through my own experience with invasive ductal carcinoma.

To the entire cancer team at Northwestern Delnor Hospital. Your constant faith and encouragement guided my path to remission. A thank-you could never express my full appreciation.

To my family, my constant source of love and beauty. I love you so very much.

And finally, to my incredible friends. I am so blessed to have such a life-giving group of people to surround me. I may see some of you often or maybe very infrequently, but your words of encouragement stay in my heart, only to grow over time. Thank you for all of your support.

Preface

I have been encouraged to begin this story by friends. So much has brought me to this very point in my life. This pause was determined long before I entered this earth. God, in his infinite wisdom, carefully crafted each event, weaving each one with grace, creating this tapestry called me.

To waste time questioning this diagnosis would be a great disservice to my faith. Why me? Why on earth not?

Invasive ductal carcinoma has become a gift to me. Looking it in the face, armed with the shield of God's love, I hope to be an example of all that is good in this world through my illness. I have become keenly aware of my blessings, the comforts I have been afforded. I have so very much to be thankful for: my family, my friends, my home, but mostly the faith I have been afforded to find solace in.

I am going to chronicle my journey on this book, not for pity or sadness but to rejoice with me in all God has given me, and as a resource for all of you to learn from and grow with.

Together, anything is possible!

All my love,
Teri

Introduction

There are many reasons one might consider when choosing to write a book, but I believe I had no choice. It was my privilege and responsibility. My story needs to be shared, not because it is mine but it is yours as well. It is every mother's, sister's, and aunt's. It is woven as intricately into the fabric of your lives as it is mine.

Breast cancer—all of you dodge the reality that it could be a part of your identity or that of a loved one.

I had spent a good portion of my career as a radiologic technologist performing mammograms. With the advent of technology, I had seen many positive strides in early detection, giving me the ability to have teaching moments with my patients. Yet for many years, it still had not touched me personally until my mother fell victim to it.

Hers was an aggressively voracious form, growing rapidly from its first indication to her timely mastectomy. So much of her breast and surrounding tissue was removed that her chest had become concave and necrotic. It was then that the surgeons took skin from her thigh and grafted it onto her chest.

I watched her suffer through chemo, radiation, and recovery from skin grafting. I drew my inspiration for my fight from her bravery and undying faith. My mother was incredible; she never uttered a complaint and instead chose to be an example for all around her. Almost exactly five years later, she came to me for her routine mammogram. Still disfigured from her prior fight, I gently positioned her for her exam.

As I waited for her films to drop out of the processor, I felt a knot in my stomach. Soon, they fell into the film tray. I tentatively picked them up, and I lost my breath. The wicked intruder had come back to torture my beautiful mother. When I returned to the room, she smiled at me and asked me what I saw. I, of course, could not tell her.

I simply said, "The radiologist will read them later today, Mom." The second time around, she chose to do nothing. She wasn't up for the fight again, and we understood. We had another year with my mom. In that time, she brought my brother and his family, as well as mine, to Disney World. It was a long-time dream of hers. She took on the Magic Kingdom like a teenager. She drank in every minute of watching her grandchildren in awe of their surroundings.

We were back in our rooms, and she was at Epcot with five little kids in tow watching the fireworks. God gave her strength and adrenaline to live those days to her fullest. When I look back at the pictures, I see her arm swollen with lymphedema and her sleeve snuggly in place. That was in June.

By the fall, her descent came rapidly, so we decided that while she still could, she would have professional photos taken with my dad. By Christmas, she was bedridden. Hospice had taken over her care, and she remained at home. It was a beautiful April day. The sun warmed the crisp spring air as I sat by her bedside. She had not spoken for days. Her eyes were closed, but she knew I was there.

I read to her from the Bible about how the Lord would raise her up on eagles' wings. As I took her hand, I whispered, "You go ahead, Mom. Dance with the angels. I will take care of Daddy." Suddenly, she raised her arms sharply over her head, her eyes opened and transfixed to the sky, and she mumbled words I could not construe. To her, they were as clear as mine. I watched in amazement as she gasped her last breath on this earth. She had given me the greatest gift one can give another—her glimpse of heaven. The next time breast cancer became a part of me was twenty-seven years later when I was told I had invasive ductal carcinoma.

As the anniversary of my mother's death approaches, I am in awe that she has been gone for twenty-six years. That is nearly half my life I have lived without her. I constantly think about the joy she would have watching my grandchildren, her great-grandchildren, at play.

Whenever I evaluate myself a grandmother, I hold myself up to her, possibly the greatest grandmother that has ever lived. She would find the extraordinary in the mundane. A cardboard box could instantly become a castle, and a paper towel roll, the magic wand, as her love, like fairy dust, would cloak us in a ribbon of magic. I feel her by my side each time I walk through the Little Traveler with my granddaughter's, navigating our way to the atrium for pie and dessert on a Saturday afternoon.

It was there she would bring my girls to teach them how to be a little lady, showing them they were totally loved and adored. I suppose I could have a level of bitterness in losing my mom when my youngest was only five. But the path she forged for me of love and faith has been carried in my heart and grows to this day. My children have incredible memories of her, as short their time with her was, because that was what she did best.

Her mere presence drew you in like a warm blanket on a cold day. It filled you, completed you, and made you feel safe. How could that ever be bittersweet?

I knew she saw the Lord, arms wide open, welcoming her into heaven. As quickly as it began, it was over. She collapsed into a peaceful rest as she gave her last breath to this world. She was gone, but not really. She very much lives in our hearts and our children's hearts. Her memories are part of her great-grandchildren's lives even though they have never met. The gift of her sweet legacy will bless us for generations.

> I watched that day as you slipped away
> Your hand fell from mine
> Heaven was in your reach.
> Suddenly I knew,
> You were never meant to be mine forever,
> Your Faith planted in my heart
> Your smile forever in my gaze.

A slim pink ribbon unites us now.
We have fought the same fight—
We prevailed.
A Child's Garden of Verses
Will lull me to sleep.
As you dance with angels
And sing to Your Lord.
A light never diminished
Arms forever felt.

Journal entry

For years of my career I performed Mammograms. Often calming women who had just found a lump, or were having anxiety because it was their first. There were times when I had to hide my own worry when I saw a mass or suspicious area on their study. This was particularly true when my own mother came to me to perform her Mammogram. She was five years out from her initial breast cancer diagnosis and had gone through a mastectomy, radiation and chemo. As those first films popped out of the processor and I held them up, my heart sank. Her cancer had returned. I quickly gathered all the strength I had, dried my tears, and attempted to put on a happy face as I returned to her. She of course asked me what I saw, but I could not tell her. Looking back, I believe she knew, I believe most women know deep down when their bodies fail them.

Last week I went in for my screening mammogram. I have had no symptoms or complaints. At the same time I had my Dexa scan, which was completely normal. My primary is so good about releasing my reports to me immediately. The next day I received my Dexa results, but nothing regarding my Mamm. The next day passed and still no report. I had now begun to get a very uneasy feeling, wondering where my report could be. Just as I was going to shoot my doctor a message, the report appeared. There were two areas of concern on my right breast with focal irregularities and architectural distortion. I needed to go back for additional imaging and an ultrasound. Right then I knew things would never be the same. I had never had an abnormal study, and I knew these findings were suspicious. For a day or so I cried, I prayed, I spoke to my Mom, hoping for clarification and what to do with this information. I of course made my appointment for follow up, and yesterday I went to the hospital. Armed with prayers of many, I was now the anxious one, I was now the one who tried to drink in every bit of information and read each line on the face of my Technologist. I was blessed with a compassionate and caring peer, because she knew my background, she invited me into every step of the imaging. And even though I asked her questions I knew she was not at liberty to answer, she kindly answered me the best she could.

After my Ultrasound, she left the room, and gave me a warm blanket. Soon after the Radiologist, The Nurse Navigator and the Ultrasound Technologist returned and crowded into the dark room. With a few more confirming swipes of Ultrasound, they asked me to sit up so they could tell me the findings. A hypoechogenic mass with irregularities and spiculated margins. Biorads 5—a malignant mass, cancer. I think I already knew, just like my Mom. God had prepared me with subtlety and love. His gentle hand had guided me to this point and will continue to do so throughout this entire journey. A certain calm washed over me knowing what I had to do. The uncertainty of the prior days was gone. Before I left, the nurse made me an appointment with a breast surgeon for next Tuesday. At that time I will undergo a core biopsy to determine the type of breast cancer I have. From there the surgical and the treatment plan will be developed.

My fervent prayer is to give my family strength. And, that I might handle this with the Grace and eloquence my Mother did. A figure of Faith, and an example of God's undying love for us.

You might wonder how I could feel Cancer could be a sign of God's love for us. Just like my Mother, he has now chosen me to be that example. My gift back to him will be the way I chose to navigate my course. And that will be with all the love and Faith that I can give. This destiny was laid out long ago, through all the years I performed Mammograms on other women, he was preparing me for this moment, this very time.

As I drove to the surgeon's office yesterday, the strength I had previously felt began to melt away. The uncertainty of my visit outweighed the knowledge I had already received. As I stepped through the doors of the Cancer Care Center, I began to feel a pang of nausea as I made my way to check in.

After what seemed like forever, a kind nurse appeared to escort me back to the exam room. She handed me a crisp cotton cape covered with flowers to change into.

As I sat waiting for the surgeon my mind went to a time when I was much younger. My beautiful blonde children laughing and playing, still needing me as children do. With eyes closed, a smile crept across my face. Watching my children run through a field, their soft hair flirting with the wind gave me peace. My daydream was suddenly interrupted by the opening of the door and my surgeon greeting me.

A woman of slight stature greeted me in a big way. She confirmed my cancer diagnosis and went on to tell me it's nature. I have Invasive Ductal Carcinoma. That is a cancer that begins in the milk ducts of the breast but has spread beyond the duct now. I am also HR positive, which isn't a good thing or a bad thing, it just helps guide the course of therapy. After much discussion and teaching on her part, it was decided I will undergo a partial right mastectomy on October 29th. They will also perform a sentinel node biopsy. It will be guided by radioactive dye that is injected during surgery. The dye will travel to the nodes and show which ones are "open" and could have cancer in them. That way they are not removing more lymph nodes than necessary and help with recovery. Post Op I will for sure be undergoing Radiation Therapy. Depending on the final Histology after surgery the question of Chemotherapy will be answered. Or, another possibility could be a five year course of a medication along the lines of Tamoxifen.

The reason I share all of this with you is to make you aware of what can happen. Never in a million years, did I think when I went in for my routine mammogram, I would be on this journey. My cancer was not palpable. I went to my doctor every year for an exam. I did routine checks on myself. If not for the advancements in Mammography from 2D to 3D Tomosynthesis, my cancer may have not been found until much later.

Please, please, be vigilant, be your best advocate. Never, ever take anything for granted.

I will continue to share my journey. And if it helps just one woman, then whatever lies ahead, will not be in vain. I don't ask why, as I shared before, this is a part of my life determined long ago.

As I sat in church on Sunday, Doug to my left and Ella to my right, my eyes were centered on the cross. Staring at Christ's face, he spoke to my heart.

At that moment it became clear.

I told our Lord, if you could do that for me (dying on the cross) I can do this for you.

Life has a habit of bringing turmoil in threes. For me, this was certainly true in 2020.

In April, I fell and suffered a significant fracture to my left ankle. For all of you familiar with medical terms, I had a trimalleolar fracture with complete lateral displacement of my foot. Part of my tibia had actually pierced my skin, making it an open fracture. I was at home, and my husband called 911 after determining it would not be prudent to move me.

I was brought to the ER where my fracture was reduced and splinted. I was admitted and underwent surgery the next day. After a couple of days in the hospital, I began to show concerning symptoms, and the day I was to be discharged, I tested positive for COVID. I was told I contracted it in the ER. You see, this was just when people were becoming keenly aware of the virus and its effects. Going into the ER with an ortho injury didn't necessitate full PPE gear. I believe masks were worn, but I had no respiratory symptoms.

I went on to spend a month in the hospital. At that time, you were not allowed visitors. I became incredibly lonely. As you know, being sick and in the hospital is hard enough, but without family, it is particularly disheartening. Everyone I came in contact with was completely covered in protective gear. My only human contact was through their eyes. Their beautiful, compassionate, caring eyes.

I truly do believe that eyes are the windows to the soul. My caregivers' eyes filled me with the power to get better and fight. It is amazing how you can adapt to a different environment, one out of the norm. God fills us with similar circumstances in your life. God steps right in and gives us the tools to cope, and he is found everywhere in the midst of disparity! Through each person who held out their hand, each new day that held the promise of hope, each whisper that fills your heart joy. That is faith; that is God!

After I came home, I was sequestered in my room for two additional weeks because of my husband's underlying conditions. Plus I had a huge cast on my legs and was nonweight bearing! I was totally dependent on others. At one point, I began to cry to my husband how horrible I felt that he had to do so much for me. He turned to me, his mouth forming an unmistakable smile, as he told me it was his privilege and honor to care for me. I was gobsmacked! Privilege and honor?

I thought about it later. That must be how God feels—we try and do things on our own, try to solve our deepest worries, never turning to ask for help. But when we finally do and surrender ourselves in exhaustion, he is right there, smiling, happy that we finally came to him. Because he is always there by our side.

I would look out the window and watch spring coming alive without me. I longed to go outside and take in the season. The hours turned to days. I missed my family terribly, but I knew I was where I needed to be. It was just my heart longed to hug my grandchildren, feel the touch of my children and husband—what everyone needs to heal.

One evening about three weeks in, I got up to go to the bathroom and became short of breath. I reached the bed and pushed the call button. I could feel my breathing becoming more and more rapid and shallow. Soon, an entourage of caregivers in full PPE surrounded me. I could see the doctor out of the corner of my eye calling the code.

Soon, my gown was being ripped off of me and replaced by electrodes. A mask covered my face, feeding me oxygen. The call was made to 911, and after I was stabilized, I was to be transported to CDH. I begged them not to send me and began to cry. I was so afraid I would be put on a ventilator and never be able to speak to my loved ones again, let alone see them. I asked them to hand me my phone so I could call Doug. I needed to at least tell him what was in my heart.

I was wheeled to the ambulance; and as I got outside, I took off the oxygen mask, breathing in God's air for the first time in twenty-one days. The clear sky was dotted with stars. I embraced it all. I drank it in as though I had just returned from a long journey, parched for its goodness. Those moments were God's promise to me that I would be okay. They were his get-well card painted in glory. And a particular peace settled within me.

I did go on to the hospital. It was there through a CT that they found the damage this virus had left on my lungs. After I went home, I was quarantined to my room for two more weeks to protect Doug.

As long as I live, I will never forget that evening or the promise God gave me through the beauty of his sky and the air that we breathe. I carry that promise with me five months later. His gentle reminders follow me each day. My family, my friends, my faith—

sometimes, they are given with a whisper, and sometimes they are shouted at me! He will never let me forget his faithfulness, not then and certainly not now.

Journal entry

No words can describe the sadness of the weeks, days, hours or minutes I have lost with you. The incredible healing of your touch, or the smiles that race across your face. This is what I hold close to my heart until I can hold you again. Until then, I scan these pictures, remembering the moments in which they were made. I gather them together, like precious pieces of my heart, holding them close, reveling in their grace and goodness. God has given so much to me, I could never consider this time what he has taken. He has given this pause for me to realize the bounty of blessings he has cloaked me with. This gift, perhaps in an unusual and unconventional box, nonetheless is just that, a gift. These moments are ours to facilitate the beauty of this time and draw from it the strength to never let ambivalence make its way back into our lives.

Until I can hold you again, I hold you in my heart and my soul!! All my love, Teri, Mom, and Grandma.

It's easy to be brave when you are blind,
Following paths not yet defined.
Holding back tears you dare not shed,
Holding onto words,
Only in your head.
Gathering up tomorrow's hidden from view,
Endlessly praying but answering a few.
Someday to break, like water from a fall,
The bricks fall down, a tumbling wall.
No longer blind, but gratefully see,
Blessings He holds, only for me.
Blind

I have been blessed with five beautiful grandchildren. Anyone who has been given even one knows what a healing effect their simple touch can have. My mom always said she lived her life to be a grandma. At a younger age, I would get a little miffed by this statement. After all, was my brother and I not a great joy to her? But as I grew older and I watched her joyfully play make-believe with my children or bring them to the circus or feed the ducks, it began to become clearer. It filled my heart to see my own children laugh with my mom or simply settle into her lap for a story.

She died far too soon, and my children were robbed of the magic that was their grandmother. My youngest, barely five, still remembers the love that was hers alone. My two older ones were eight and twelve. Their memories are much more vivid and plentiful. So many times as I watch my own grandchildren play, I close my eyes and wish she was here to be a part of their lives. She would relish being a great-grandma!

It is now her words that have come full circle for me. I realize what she meant when she said he lived her life to be a grandma, as I am a grandma myself. With your own children, it is your responsibility to discipline them, nurture them, and guide them to be their best possible selves. As a grandparent, you augment those values, but you are able to enjoy the unbridled purity of their love. And that joy transcends everything, even cancer!

She nestled in so close, I could hear her breathe. Rhythmically, lulling me into a gentle peace, the way only Ella Grace could do.

I am in my 2nd week of treatment. The fatigue they warn about has settled in and taken up my reserve. I have learned whatever I want to accomplish, I must complete in the morning. Each morning I wake and ready to tackle the day. But, by the time afternoon is upon me, I begin my descent into lethargy. By the time I return from treatment, it's all over. And so, when I returned home yesterday I laid in my bed, and closed my eyes. Soon, I felt her next to me. She just crawled in next to me as though she knew how much I needed her. That simple act of laying quietly next to me, filled me with a healing hope. The love she shared without a word surrounded my heart giving me strength. She knew what I needed, and so did God when he blessed our family with her sweet soul.

There are so many people I have met on this journey and even more who have entered my life in silence, each of them with their unique struggle—some with diminished bodies, struck by the ravages of cancer—and then there are some much like me. It is hard to tell they are engaged in a battle at all. But all of them have a story to tell. Sometimes, just a word can open a much-needed conversation. I offer a prayer to all. And then I thank God for all he has given me.

Not everyone has an Ella Grace to hold. So I will take what she gives me and pass it on. After all, at the end of the day, I can lay down and gather more, recharging me for the day to come.

Today I had the honor of taking my sweet Natalee for her locker set up the second year in a row. Today looked a bit different than last year, but the building was brimming with excitement nonetheless. As I watched her place her essentials in her locker, I couldn't help but reminisce about just how far she has come. The countless years, months, weeks and hours of Occupational, Speech and Physical therapy seemed insurmountable to her 2 year old spirit. She didn't realize she had Autism, only that her world seemed much different than ours. I can only imagine how frightening that must have been, especially without words to communicate. It wasn't until she was 4 that she could put 2 words together, always in the third person. The melt downs that love could not heal, a prisoner of ambivalence, she never wanted to be held. How I longed for her to understand just how much I loved her, and waited for a sign that she loved me. Through the years she began to grow, like a beautiful butterfly, she finally took to her wings. At first, small journeys, gradually awakening, Natalee began to break away from the cocoon of Autism that held her, as today she takes flight and soars. My honor roll student, smiling at classmates in the hallway, initiating conversations, and taking in all of the correct social cues. My heart is so full of love for her. Her perseverance, strength, and beauty.

As tradition would have it, we made our way to Starbucks afterwards. We sat, talked, giggled and spent a wonderful afternoon together!

Finding her locker was amazing, watching her interact with her peers, I was filled with thanks, laughing together in the drive thru; Priceless, truly priceless.

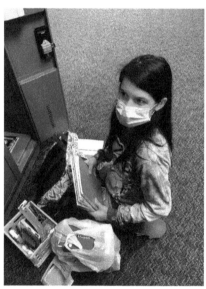 

During a cancer diagnosis or any other significant event in your life, God will play a very important role.

I have a group of women that I meet with on Tuesday mornings. We are diverse in many ways but rooted in a great love of God. We come from different faith walks but are bound by the words of scripture. These women have been with me through more obstacles in my life than I can even remember, as well as when my cancer diagnosis was a given.

Finding a spiritual hub, a grounded environment that can lift you out of darkness or carry you in joy, has been the cornerstone of my recovery. We have shared intimate details of our lives that have only been expressed in the walls of our meetings. I have ugly cried, and they were there wiping my tears. I have laughed myself into an asthma attack with them, and they were there with my inhaler and water. To call this sorority of faith a blessing would be a great understatement.

You need to feed your soul with the goodness of his grace! My mother's source of nourishment is mass. I am a Catholic Christian. Born into the faith at a time in my life I have taken it for granted, not always realizing the healing power of the Eucharist, I think I had to have those lapses of apathy to fully understand how very much every way I govern my life was met through the Spirit.

My love for God has gradually grown until he now fills every aspect of my life, including my cancer diagnosis. I have grown to realize what a blessing it has been in my life. The love and support I have received has brought me to my knees in thanks. As many of you know, spend a day in a cancer center and walk away grateful for all of you have been spared.

Faith and dealing with disease should be synonymous. You can't do the dealing without the faith. For us now, it looks a bit different: churches at 25 percent capacity, fellow congregants in masks, no choirs. But I say this to you as sure as anything that the most important component is still there—God. And he is ready to meet you and make you whole again.

Journal entry

The alarm went off yesterday as I rolled over settling into my soft comforter. It seemed the perfect morning to stay in bed, taking in the gloomy skies. I've heard that voice inside me before urging me to ignore what I need, depriving my soul of needed nourishment.

Tuesday is my ladies prayer group/bible study. These incredible women have supported me through some of my greatest challenges. They always reel me in, giving the gift of importance to me. Our meetings signal calm and peace in me, yesterday was no exception.

As we immersed ourselves in Romans, God's words quickly filled me. Paul in his writings reminds us of Christ's sacrifice to heal us from sin, and our direct obligation to never take that for granted. It certainly isn't our hall pass.

But in a keener sense I re-examined what that means in relationship to me and my Cancer.

If God asked his own son to be crucified in the human sense, how much must he love me to trust me with this moment. Think about what Christ gave to us, with dignity, love, and acceptance. I must humbly try in some small way to mirror his sacrifice, revealing Gods enduring love for us. I am brought to my knees in gratitude for this opportunity as well as all of the blessings that have filled my life.

My road is just opening, I tread softly and carefully. May I be just what our Lord wants me to be. May I be his voice on earth. May I be a conduit of his Grace and his love.

After meeting with my Tuesday Morning Ladies yesterday, I realized that I had not yet processed my cancer. Truthfully, I hadn't had the time. With a whirlwind of surgery and treatments my focus was being strong and going forward for my family. Now that the dust has settled so to speak, I have the luxury to grieve, discern, and look towards my new normal. Left alone with my thoughts, I wrote this poem.

Journey

Tears fall to stain my face,
Creases given for your Grace.
A hollowed spirit onto pass Joy,
slipping from a grasp.
Behold these hands clenched in prayer,
Knees bent over in despair.
Voices sent with one implore,
heaven's door.
Beam of Grace fill my soul,
Tender hope beat untold.
Healing comes oh strands of light,
No longer burdened—no longer fight.
Mother Peace, love to spare—
Joy is mine—beyond compare.
Tac

There will be times you doubt God's presence during this time, and that's okay. Jesus himself asked his father, "My God, why have you forsaken me?"

We are only human! There are so many thoughts racing through your mind, not only regarding yourself but your family. I know for a long time I was on autopilot. I was so busy trying to be brave and to forget through for those I loved that I have little thought to my own feelings. I suspect many handle it the same way, although looking back, I don't think it was the smartest way to deal with things. Sooner or later, those latent emotions have to surface.

For me, small things became insurmountable. I would cry if we were out of milk! Sobbing, I would question, how are we going to get more? A bit dramatic, I concede, but it was very real to me at the time.

It is through doubt that we find our heart. We have to question our place in his plan for us, and then we need to sit back and listen. Really listen to the words your life is scripting for you. Cancer is a stepping stone to greater destiny and our path to service for others.

My writing has been confined to emails, a blog, and the confines of Facebook. But through my examination of the total landscape of my cancer, I listened. Slowly but surely, my friends and family encouraged me to share my writings and my experience through a book. I thought to myself, *No one wants to read about this. My friends and family have an inflated opinion of my literary talents.* But I suppose if you are reading this, I did the right thing!

At the beginning of my diagnosis, I told God, "If you could die on the cross, I can do this for you and for your Glory." So each day I aspire to carry out that promise, even now after surgery and treatment. The way I govern myself with this will be an example to my daughters and granddaughters, just like my mom did for me. And that is an awesome responsibility that God trusted you with because he loves you that much!

As I hurried to get ready for my lymph-edema appointment this morning, my clumsy self fell over my boots and into my dresser.

As I stood next to this obtrusive piece of furniture, my head buried in my arm, I began to cry. *Please, God, don't let me fall again. Please, God, I just can't. I can't do it right now!* The weakness of my words echoed through me as the tears fell through the creases of my face.

All at once, I gathered my thoughts, wiped my tears, and stood up. How could I doubt that he knows what is best for me? He is always at my side, never failing, never ceasing to love me with a love I could only imagine. I could hear my heart pounding and, with each beat, a resonant reminder of my ill-forgotten faith.

I think that sometimes, during our difficult moments, we tend to lose sight of what we know best. Ever since my cancer diagnosis, he has shown me over and over again the magnificence of his love. I have been given incredible support and understanding by not only friends and family but by virtual strangers. The prayers and well wishes have brought me to my knees. An abundance of grace that could only be orchestrated by our God.

Please pray for my family, especially Doug, during this difficult time. I firmly believe it is much more difficult for families than it is for the patient. As always, I'm grateful for all I have been given, now and always.

I just received my call from the hospital. My surgery is scheduled for 1:30 tomorrow. I am oddly at peace with it, so much so I am surprising myself. But, with the guidance of prayer, I have done something I normally don't do, at least not easily. I have put it totally in God's hands. Not that I haven't done this before, but in my impatient heart, I usually yank it back, foolishly thinking I am back in control! Ha! I am in control…

Thankfully, my heart has slowed down, taken in the moment, and allowed God's Grace to guide me. I know, he is in control, and I'm happy to hand over the wheel.

I need to soak in the beauty of these next few days. His goodness brought me to his arms, sheltered in the shadow of heaven.

I will keep you all updated. Thank you for your prayers, your love, and your support.

With Gratitude, Teri.

I remember the day vividly. The sky was a perfect shade of blue, and the sun draped across the landscape unapologetically. It was the type of day poems are composed. It wasn't just because I was going home from the hospital, but the cancer had been removed from my body.

I had to stay a couple of extra days due to blood pressure issues. Otherwise, I would have gone home the same day as my surgery as I am sure many of you have. I had the choice between a mastectomy and a partial mastectomy. My surgeon reassured me there was no difference in longevity with either surgery, so I opted for the partial.

I sport a six-inch incision about five centimeters above my nipple where they removed the cancer and surrounding tissue. I also have a six-inch incision laterally below my axilla where they removed my lymph nodes. Truth be told, the latter has been the most bothersome. It seems as though everything rubs against it and bothers it! Small price to pay for the end result.

I had such a feeling of freedom after the cancer was removed, like a nagging mole removed from your face. I felt whole and beautiful again. I gave little thought to what lay ahead: treatments, daily provisions, doctor's visits, and fatigue. Oh man, fatigue.

You will soon know, if you don't already, whatever inconvenience you may encounter, it won't matter. The prize in the end is your life. The inexplicable beauty afforded you as a child of God—life! I relied heavily on prayer and meditation during this time, immersing myself in the peace only the Spirit can give, whether this be quietly listening to music, reading, or creating a dialogue with God. It is essential to have that time to regroup, listen to your heart, and heal. Be kind to yourself, be patient with yourself, and never lose sight of the greater good ahead.

The sun has never been brighter, or the trees more beautiful. Like a picture postcard, I celebrated the season as Doug drove me home. Today is a perfect fall day! When I think of my favorite season, this is the picture painted in my mind. A subtle gift from heaven. I vow to be open to all the gifts I have been given, large and small! I think when you face a health crisis, your senses become keenly aware of all that you have. The mundane becomes extraordinary, the simple imitates complexity. Joy shouts louder, prayers are more intimate. It is God's whisper, telling me everything is well. My job is just maintaining an open heart, so I may be filled with certain Grace.

Thank you for all of your support and prayers. I carry them with me, always, inside of my heart. I couldn't do this without each of you, you mean so very much to me. Now and always.

Journal entry

Today as I was getting ready I looked in the mirror. Staring back at me, two fresh incisions. The scars that would save my life. My scars are nothing special. I join so many warriors and brave women whose scars might mirror mine. Born from the bravery one is forced to accept.

My tears are generic in this sorority of fighters. They have been shed across the millions of faces who now stand proudly as survivors. My prayers are heard in the same voice as theirs. Sisters I will never meet, bound by the DNA of cancer. My joy is the same joy as countless women who hear the words, your margins are clean, your lymph nodes look good.

And so I will celebrate these scars, they lead to the definition of my new normal. Along the way I will carry those too weary to walk and hold them up in prayer. I will stand beside my new found sisterhood and give life to finding a cure, for one, perhaps for all.

My scars are not special, they help to tell a very special story. They are not special, but they are mine.

Like so many, my emotions ran the gamut during my breast cancer. There were times I was very optimistic, but there were also times I would look at myself as an outright pity party. After a sufficient time, I would wipe my face, blow my nose, and circle back to reality.

There is nothing wrong for mourning what was your "normal" life. The key is not to dwell on it and let it swallow you up! Embrace your new normal! There truly is so much to be grateful for. There have been so many strides in treatment for breast cancer. In fact, when I was finished with treatment, I actually sat back and marveled. Was this all there was to it?

It was nearly anticlimatic, if that makes any sense. When I would return to the cancer center to follow up, I felt guilty looking around at so many others who were suffering in imaginable ways, curled in their wheelchairs but still keeping all hope alive. If I was to have cancer, why did God spare me from their destiny? My reflections brought me to the conclusion that I was to show his healing glory through my journey. And that began with Facebook postings, blogs, and now this very book.

I used to get frustrated with my sweet husband who took to treating me like a china doll, as though I would break with the least of physical movements. And I would turn to him and say, "Please, honey, if I have the energy, allow me to do this! I need to do it!" Even now, five months later, he guards my actions carefully! He really is quite content having me sit at a desk and type on my laptop! Don't give up and don't give in! Keep up the good fight. You are worth it.

The unknown is always so very scary. Chances are, this is the greatest health crisis you have ever faced. This is all new to you. Let the seeds of doubt give the way to faith. Your tears can cultivate a new beginning. Let your very surrender to his will cloak you in his ever-present grace.

Journal entry

When I began this blog, I promised myself I would share my whole journey, not just the good and not just the bad.

Unfortunately today I am having a tough time. The incision that goes laterally and under my arm is so exquisitely tender, it has brought me to tears. Everything rubs against it, causing repeated irritation. This is the incision for the sentinel node biopsy and lymph node dissection. Truth be told I'm tired of being sick. This has been a year long experience between my ankle fracture and surgery, then Covid and now Breast Cancer. I know I really have no room to complain, it just worries me what my poor family has been going through, especially Doug.

This is just a bump in the road, a long road that lies ahead.

Journal entry

I haven't written in a while because I have been in a holding pattern of sorts. I do have some news now that I can share.

Friday, I went back to see the surgeon. They are very pleased with my healing incisions. It was explained to me that the surgeon now takes a back seat once the cancer is removed. Barring any complications, I won't see her again for another 4 months.

Today, I had the privilege of seeing my incredible medical Oncologist. I will admit while I waited in the pale yellow exam room, my anticipation gave way to anxiety. As my stomach churned for the 25th time, the door opened, and in walked an amazing physician and man. He went on to spend an hour and a half with me. He explained treatment options and what he felt was best for me. We also discovered we had common Faith. From there I was able to communicate not only my physical concerns, but how my Faith entered into my Cancer journey. What a blessing to be able to share such a huge part of myself with my doctor! We ended our appointment by him telling me, I do what I can to heal a patient, and then I pray that God will give them His Healing Grace. I'm so at peace with any decision he will make. It has been decided I will be on a 5 year course of estrogen blocking oral chemo. My cancer feeds off of estrogen and counts on it for the cells to grow and divide. So, with this medication all estrogen is blocked before it can reach the cells to grow. From my pathology it was determined there were actually 3 types of cancer present. My overall diagnosis is still Invasive Ductal Carcinoma. But there was Ductal Carcinoma in situ and Lobular Carcinoma present. The Lobular is an indication that my breast tissue is "misbehaving" and prone to developing cancer again. This medication again, will stop it in its tracks.

My case was presented at The Tumor Conference in the hospital today. My doctor was able to tell me I will begin Radiation Therapy the week after Thanksgiving. When that has ended, I will wait two weeks and then begin the oral chemo.

I will be seeing the Radiation Oncologist tomorrow and learn more about my treatment then.

I also need to see the Geneticist. Because of having a history of early hysterectomy as well as being adopted, and a questionable health history, my doctor wants me to be tested for the Brca gene. If I have it, he will suggest I have a double mastectomy with reconstruction. And, of course my daughters would then be tested. They will be calling me for an appointment.

I am so thankful for this incredible sense of peace that has fallen over me. It has given me the eyes to see all I have been given and be thankful for it. It has provided me a heart to give and receive prayer, open to the intercessions that I am blessed with. It has given me the strength to accept what lies ahead and hold it in blind faith.

Thank you for continuing this journey with
me, each step is an affirmation toward a cure.

I was fortunate enough to not require chemotherapy. My breast cancer was HR positive and HER2 negative. Chemotherapy would have done nothing for my cancer. My tumor was removed via surgery and was found to feed off hormones. The mission was to destroy any remaining cells via radiation therapy and block hormones through a five-year course of Letrozole. Now if you google Letrozole, it is listed as an oral chemotherapy, not in a traditional infusion sense but through a daily oral pill.

Being a radiologic technologist for thirty-five-plus years, I thought very little about the effects of radiation therapy. After all, radiation had been a part of my everyday life for many years. I had a rough idea what it entailed. Oh what an inflated picture I had painted of my limited knowledge.

For me, it was complete surrender! Surrender to modesty and surrender of my trust as I laid on the table that very first day. Completely exposed from the waist up while the radiation oncologist and three techs circled around was a sobering experience.

After having three children and multiple surgeries, it had been a very long time since I considered myself modest. But there I was like a blushing bride on her wedding night, looking for any way to cover up, when they had finished mapping me for my treatments. I sat up, took in a deep breath, and said, "Lord, let it be your will." And with that, an air of contentment washed over me, and I was renewed.

I immediately began joking with the techs about the purple marks that were splattered across my chest, asking if I could connect the dots, color them in, or change the color to suit my apparel. And just like that, the mood was lightened.

Never take yourself too seriously! When I say laughter is the best medicine, this is not just a cliché. If you can find some joy in the tragedy, it will never bury you in a morose abyss. You will *always* be above it!

Journal entry

Today was hard. It was far more emotional than I had ever begun to imagine. Today I had the mapping and planning session for my Radiation Therapy. From the beginning of this journey I have been blessed with an extraordinary sense of peace. Never once have I doubted that my health would not be restored. I have met with surgeons, oncologists and geneticists. I have had surgery and sported my scars. These encounters were always a part of my resolve.

But today, it really slapped me in the face with the reality of my situation. As I laid on the CT table, my gown gathered at my waist, with my chest fully exposed. My hands were put above my head, the pain rang through my right arm like a dagger. I was to remain perfectly still for 20 minutes while they mapped out where the Radiation beam would enter me. I was informed this would be the position I would be in for all of my treatments.

As they marked my chest with a permanent pen to guide them in the future, I felt vulnerable. A vulnerability I had never experienced before. A vulnerability birthed from complete surrender. Carried in the knowledge that I couldn't possibly control my circumstances.

It was a different surrender than the day I surrendered my cancer to God. That was like having a weight lifted, giving me the grace to have absolute peace. I knew I needed that once again. As the machine carried me in and out of the CT, I closed my eyes, took in deep breaths, and listened for guidance. A long awaited message settled in my ear "Be still, Be still, and know that I am your God" the most gracious words, in one of my most difficult moments. I felt my body deflate into certain relaxation and my peace was restored.

After the session I returned to the dressing room. As I walked into the waiting room I met a woman who appeared younger than me perhaps by 10 years or so. There is no small talk, or polite niceties shared in a waiting room filled with cancer patients. I looked at her, smiled beneath my mask, and we began to talk. We are both breast cancer patients. But as we began to share details, much like some women exchange recipes, I was reminded again how blessed I am. She had undergone chemo prior to her surgery. Thankfully her body responded. I looked at her, noticing her beautiful blond hair, but that was a facade, a cruel fatality of chemo. She had lost all of hair, and her hair was a wig. I am just beginning the treatment she is almost half way through.

For that brief interlude of time, I felt an incredible kinship. And although much of our conversation consisted of mere glances of compassion through the brow of our masks, I felt her heart, and I believe she felt mine. As the nurse ushered me away I turned to say goodbye, and she gestured a wave and a smile.

I know I will be fine, all will be well, because
I know my God, and I know he is so very good. I
just need to be still and listen.

My radiation therapy began the Monday after Thanksgiving. Between my mapping and therapy, I had a bit of a reprieve.

This past Thanksgiving had a particular joy to it this year. I was so thankful to be alive! I had no idea cancer was hiding in the shadows of my right breast. I had gone in for a routine mammogram. There were no palpable masses, and my doctor didn't even feel anything. It was by God's grace it was found at all.

It was found early and taken care of expeditiously.

I had two weeks to drink in my family. And with a grateful heart, I counted each and every blessing. The smallest fraction of my life now carried the greatest sum. I found incredible comfort in my home, the softness that filled every inch. Food tasted better, and I had a keen sense that I was the luckiest woman in the world.

I couldn't help but think, why did it take a dance with fate for me to appreciate all I have been given? Not just now, but every day. Do you ever sit back and just soak it all in? All that you have and been given. I think in this kaleidoscope of life, we become so preoccupied with our lives it becomes a given. It is taken for granted we have a home for our family, food in our cupboard, heat in the winter, cooling in the summer, and a television to watch our news on.

Take a moment, close your eyes, and take it in—the sweetness of God's enduring love.

Journal entry

No doctors appointments, no treatments, nothing this week but family! I did get a call from my geneticist, I tested negative for the BRCA gene mutation, as well as 42 other possible pre-dispositions to cancer and other diseases. So, my cancer is not hereditary. That is good news for my girls, but, they still need to be vigilant as it doesn't erase the fact that I do have breast cancer, and they are genetically bound to me.

I truly feel compelled to share my grati-tude this Thanksgiving. My family, my friends, my Faith, have all been out front and center for me to hold near. These days when the food lines stretch for miles, and Covid rages on, jobs are being lost, and people's homes are in peril, my heart aches. When I look at all I have been given, all that I have, I feel humbled, but at a loss. I wish I could vanquish the pain that looms over so many, but all I have is prayer.

When I look in the mirror, and see the changes my body is going through, they pale in comparison to so many. And so, I will offer any pain or discomfort I may have to God, and ask that he eases another's. Perhaps someone might find peace. The peace that settles in like a warm blanket on a snowy night. A peace that will warm them like the crackling embers of a fire. A peace that will feed them like turkey and dressing, and fill them until they find rest.

My miracles surround me, my eyes are open. My prayer is that yours are too.

We twirled effortlessly across the living room floor. Ella's soft sweet head grazed my cheek as Barbra Streisand serenaded us. Outside, the leaves and wind did their obligatory Fall tango, as the sun drenched us in warmth. In this moment, one could not have been more thankful to be alive. A moment in my obtrusive despair, I would forever reference. So many times I feel we let these moments go unnoticed, lost in the abyss of our daily lives. Instead, they should become our prayer, tucked in the recesses of our soul. How thankful so many of us should be.

The next time I peer into the pantry and announce, there is nothing to eat! I will think about the ones who go to sleep with bloated bellies and dry eyes, from hunger and dehydration.

When I crawl into the sea of goose down in my bed at night, and exclaim, it is too hot in here may I remember those who live in alleyways and under bridges with nothing but the crude accessory of a cardboard box to keep them warm at night.

When I look at my bank account and feel cheated because "I am Broke" May I remember those who are truly penniless, fighting to survive each moment of their lives.

I know for certain, I have been entrusted as the steward of immeasurable wealth. Not monetary wealth, but that of trusted friends, loving family, and Faith.

Please examine your own wealth this Thanksgiving, and find joy in the special moments that will soon be prayer. All of you have blessed me in my life. And for that privilege I will give thanks. Not just on Thanksgiving, but each and every day!

I was so busy plowing through what I thought I was expected to do I had little time for raw emotion. After all, that would signal a weakness or a vulnerability. I was supposed to be a strong, resilient woman, and that didn't fit the model. Maybe I was afraid if I let that little crack of insecurity in, I would be opening a floodgate I didn't have the strength to fix.

Whatever the reason, it felt oddly uncomfortable and almost inhuman. Who doesn't break down when given a cancer diagnosis? I would, for one, and I'm sure many of you as well. Perhaps God invokes this mechanism to protect us. Like adrenaline and shock when you have a trauma protects you from the severity of your pain, the inability to cry protects you from the severity of your pain; the inability to cry protects you from the severity of your diagnosis.

I'm not sure if my lack of tears was good or bad, only that I had wished for a long time I could cry. I thought that release would make me feel "normal." I seriously thought there was something wrong with me.

Time would go on to prove that was not the case. There is no script to follow. There are no secrets to unfold. Follow your heart and put your faith in God. He will be your guide always.

I haven't cried yet. I have shed a few tears from time to time, but I haven't had that watershed moment. The realization that stirred within me like a cyclone of emotions brimming forward into the consummate release. It has not come. It gives me pause, wondering why.

When my parents died I had the same reaction. I watched them die over the months that preceded their actual death. It was absolutely no surprise, and I knew they would finally be at peace in a much better place.

And so I have to question my lack of tears related to my peace I have within for this circumstance? Because much like I gave my parents and their pain to God, I did the very same thing after I received my diagnosis. I left it in his Hands, and He has carried me.

I still feel like I have something in me that needs to be released. There is an uneasy heaviness on my heart that I think would feel so much better, if only I could cry.

This could all change tomorrow or at any given moment. My emotions run the gamut, and like a roller coaster can be soaring high, or falling into a steep fall.

I begin my radiation therapy tomorrow and I'm sure the newness and unfounded direction of the day will lend itself to a vulnerability, one of which I have never experienced.

But tomorrow is tomorrow and today I do nothing but look forward, always and predictably forward.

Undergoing the daily ritual of treatment can be taxing both mentally and physically. For me, my radiation treatments were every day for five weeks. They were scheduled at the same time each day, and they became as much a part of me as brushing my teeth.

I grew to know my therapists, nurses, and office personnel quite well. I was even on a first-name basis with the valet. Those people there, by circumstance, became family by choice. Their unselfish love propels you into recovery.

I want to tell you a story about one of my therapists. He was a handsome young man in his thirties. He was kind and compassionate. His eyes told the story of a maturity beyond his years. One day, I asked about his family. He told me about his wife and three beautiful daughters. The middle daughter was just six. He went on to tell me of the special relationship he had with her.

At age three, she was diagnosed with leukemia. For the past three years, she battled it bravely and was now in remission. Think about it. Only three years old! She had been on chemotherapy for three years, her tiny body in the fight of her life. And her dad treated cancer patients every day with radiation.

Never did he lose his dedication to others while his baby girl fought to live. Instead, I believe it made him more dedicated to his craft. It empowered his very belief in miracles. God places him exactly where he needed him to give hope. My eyes filled with tears trying to imagine the magnitude of his gift. When he told the story, there wasn't a hint of pity or sadness, only gratitude and love.

I know we are all put on this earth to be of service to each other. The people that you encounter throughout your life are not by accident or coincidence. Each of them is placed on your journey for you to teach or for them to teach you a very valuable lesson to promote your growth.

And so it was for me that day, what a beautiful lesson it was.

The ceiling tiles are made to look as though you are looking out a window on a sunny day. The vivid blue sky, a spattering of clouds, all meant to ease and console. Just as I begin to get lost in the imagery, the gantry moves, obstructing my view, and reeling me back into what is real.

As I lay on the hard table, my arms uncomfortably positioned above my head, radiation in greater volumes than I ever delivered streaming across my marked chest, I close my eyes, breathing in and out with deliberation praying to relax. To transport yourself to a different place, a happy place, is the key to lying still, perfectly still. The therapy is delivered in such precise mm measurements. One flinch could uproot the entire session.

I am already weary of my daily ritual. Tired of my life mapped out around my trip to the cancer center. In those moments I lose sight of the greater good. The days, weeks, months and years this will afford me to watch my grandchildren grow. The seasons I will experience. First snowfalls I will be able to inhale, fall leaves I will kick through. The first breath of Spring, and long summer nights that never seem to sleep. This is all mine, for 30 minutes of inconvenience.

Really, who am I to complain? Rather I should fall to my knees and thank God for this minor intrusion into my life.

I am the lucky one, I am the bold one, I am a survivor!

Father God,

You are the creator of all. You love each of us, we are but a line in the palm of your hand.

Our journey was given to us long before our birth. You knew each step, each breath we would breathe, each beat our heart would give.

May I glorify your loving grace on earth through my thoughts, prayers and actions. May you become a part of me, as I am of you.

Many others have a much more difficult course. May I lift them spiritually and through prayer, ever mindful of your will.

I share this prayer with those yet unknown to me, with their hearts filled with openness and gratitude fill them with your unsparing Grace.

Holy Spirit speak to us, guide us, and keep us ever close to your word.

As I enter into the end of my third week of Radiation Treatments, I have had a lot of time to reflect on my journey. My cancer pales in comparison to so many. The people I see wrought with pain, unable to walk, their eyes looking hollow with grief, surround me each day I enter the Cancer Center. I can't help but wonder why I have been spared the agony of my counterparts. I can only believe it is to be of service to these people as well as all that come into my life. I pray that I can be an example to my children and grandchildren. To show them you can be faced with adversity, and handle it with Grace, in the end be strengthened by it. I have felt from the onset of my diagnosis that God had a very specific reason for putting this in my life. Since I heard the first words spoken, I have actively prayed for him to use this to his Glory. Surprisingly, I have been at peace from the start, always feeling in my heart that I would be just fine. Physically, I have radiation burns on my chest now. And each time I go in for treatment I know it's only going to get worse before it gets better. I just keep reminding myself as I lay there, it is a small price to pay for the rest of my life. The Cancer Care center is not filled with morose people, rather I find it as a place of hope, and healing peace. I feel centered there, I know the people are there for me. I walk in the door and the receptionist knows my name. She always calls out to me as I enter the door. I have had beautiful in depth conversations with nurses, Techs, doctors and patients. There is so much joy sandwiched in an ominous facade. I'm so very thankful for all this chapter in my life has brought. The new friendships, the pain, the staff, and the million little lessons it has brought me. God works in mysterious ways. For me, he certainly does, mysterious and wonderful.

This was the last ornament to be placed on the tree and the newest one for our home. The simple message, just one word, has been the anchor of my life the past few months. The ornament was gifted to me by a not-for-profit organization called Ignite Hope. Its mission was to encourage and assist cancer patients.

As I walked out of treatment a week or so before Christmas, I was given a gift bag. Inside this beautiful ornament, a hand-poured soy candle contained a message of encouragement. The messages, wrapped in foil, presented themselves as the candle burned. And a bag of lemon heads. They erase the strange taste and dryness you can get in your mouth during treatment.

This beautiful gesture, made by complete strangers, is another example of the blessings that have been showered on me since my diagnosis. I may have put the ornament away, but its message will always be with me.

Journal entry

It came! The gut wrenching, heart aching cry finally came!

And you know what? It came at a very unexpected time and place!

So thankful was I that it wasn't in the middle of the grocery store, but within the safety of the cancer center.

"Oh Holy Night" has always been my favorite Christmas song. It, in and by itself can evoke a steady stream of tears. This past Christmas was no exception.

I sat in the waiting room waiting for my treatment, and over my head this beautiful song began to play. Alone, I closed my eyes, thinking of Christmas in the past, and Christmas in the future. I was filled with such a sense of God's love. The words hung on me like ornaments on a tree. "Oh Night Divine!" I finally felt permission to release, and by the time they had come to get me for my treatment I was in full blown ugly cry. The tech wasn't quite sure what to make of it. In between my soulful sobs I reassured him I was ok. This was ok. This was a very long time in coming.

The next day when I arrived for treatment my tech told me that he had said a prayer for me and for my family that night when he went home.

I can't remember a time I was more touched by a relative stranger.

He was no longer a stranger, but a friend. And I had been blessed, so very blessed.

I have waited, sometimes with patience, sometimes in disbelief. Waiting for that gut wrenching ugly cry to come. Today was the day as I sat waiting to be called for my treatment. "Oh Holy Night" filled the room, and suddenly before I even knew it, it was there. Like a tsunami of emotion, grief, and questions, it flooded me in unrelenting fashion. The spirit of the season, as it is for so many, bounced back and forth in my mind. It vacillated between gratitude, and longing for a Christmas past.

I was angry at myself for giving in to my sadness. I have been trying so hard to be strong, now that stiff upper lip quivered with the desire to be healthy. Tomorrow my children and grandchildren will be gathering for their annual Christmas Cookie party. Baking recipes from our parents and our own. I won't be attending this year because the fatigue has gotten the best of me. It's my trade off to be sure I can enjoy Christmas Day with my family. Skipping this tradition had weighed heavy on my heart, but, I know if I do this now, next year will be a certainty.

I am rounding the finishing line for my radiation, after next week, my daily trips will end. Left behind, will be reminders of this life saving therapy. The radiation burns could leave scars, peeling skin or blisters. The marks across my chest marking the direction of the beam will slowly fade. I've been told the fatigue could last 3 months or more. I will be well into my dosing of Letrozole by then, and onto the next step in this process.

I will always remember this Christmas and the incredible Healthcare workers that have come into my life. The ones who held my hand and reaffirmed my fears. The gazing compassionate eyes that peered beyond their masks and into my heart. Strangers who became family as they walked me through the greatest health crisis of my life.

Their mere presence is my greatest gift. Not found under a tree, but in a Cancer Center.

Yes, there is an ending to treatment! But when it ends, you, of course, are relieved. You may also be met with several other emotions.

Gratitude for your caregivers, I would assume, being right up there.

I had both of those, yet I also felt rather unsettled. The flurry of cancer treatment was now over. My daily visits to the cancer center would gradually become further and further apart.

This journey had defined me. Granted, even for only a few short months, it was ingrained in me, planted in me, and it had settled in me.

How was I to just let go as if nothing had happened? I felt lost, cast aside like a toy a child had lost interest in. It wasn't through the actions of others; please don't misunderstand this. It was all inside of me.

You may feel this was in some small way, or perhaps not at all. Remember, there are no scripts! No right or wrong. I am just sharing my experience in hopes it may help you in some small way.

The next two pages are journal entries I made after my treatment ended. They will give you a glimpse into my emotions.

Thankfulness should be the overall emotions as you will be on your way to the restoration of your health. Once you get to this point, bravo! You are a resilient survivor.

Today I had my last radiation treatment. It was met with relief, as well as sadness. This may sound strange to many, but my treatments have become a part of me. A virtual roadmap to my recovery. And all of the people I met along the way, true companions in every sense of the word. Not just caregivers but friends. As I have said before, The Cancer Center is not a morose place, but a place of peace and hope. This is remarkably due to the staff. I must say I'm left wondering what comes next. I know I will be attending a class on Survivorship. I have follow up appointments as well as beginning Letrozole on January 11th.

The imprints left on my heart from this will live long after my burns heal, the swelling leaves, and my scars begin to fade. This therapy didn't just save my life, it saved my spirit. It destroyed my cancer, but renewed my Faith. So as I left, I took with me the many little lessons afforded me, and took them in like warm soup on a snowy day. They will fill me, and sustain me as I step forward in my journey.

As I dove home God showered me with gentle reminders of his goodness and love. A sign at the church I pass that reads "Keep God Close." Further down the road a flag waved in the wind proudly displaying a cardinal. Across the street a lawn sign read "Hope is not cancelled." To me, he was sending me a love letter of hope and healing. Gently guiding me down the street to receive it, just as he has guided me through my diagnosis, surgery, and treatments. Today was not the end to my story, but rather an incredible beginning.

February 28, 2021

For so long I wondered why I didn't or couldn't cry. The year 2020 was a blur of hospitalizations, fractures, surgeries, pandemics, a life changing diagnosis's for me. One came on the cusp of the other, never really giving me the opportunity to digest the changes that were coming about in my life and body. Like a flurry of relentless blowing snow, things mounted, and mounted till I could no longer see the horizon. It's easy to be brave when you're blinded. Your adrenaline pushes you forward, and onward you follow, doing what you need to do to survive. Never once did I have a doubt I would be okay, a Grace that God had showered me with during this tumultuous storm. My Faith like a beacon, a light in the distance, comforting me and guiding me.

But now, the dust has settled and I feel more lost than ever. The chaos was the catalyst that propelled my life. It gave me purpose. Now, I am grounded on an island. An island void of treatments, surgeries, and unknown direction. I have lived through my diagnosis, my surgery, and radiation therapy. My burns have healed and blisters are gone. I am left with scars and questions. What am I now? Am I considered a survivor? Or, do I have to wait for the 5 year course of Letrozole to finish? Am I still considered a breast cancer patient? Like the air let out of a balloon I am shriveled and empty. The tears come frequently, and do not leave me feeling vindicated.

Please don't misunderstand me, I'm so thankful my health is being restored. Every day I feel stronger! But this limbo of uncertainty is a lonely place to be. It has drained my strength and determination. This truly is not a sprint, but a marathon. What physically changes you, stirs your mind and your heart. The solstice of my illness has past, perhaps the spring will forever be my new beginning.

One night after my treatment was over, my thirty-one-year-old son came to me filled with a sense of anger.

He felt that God didn't listen to him. Taken aback, I looked at him in sadness. "Why do you feel that way, Matthew?" I asked.

I should begin by telling you my journey with breast cancer was a mere blip in what I can only describe as a challenging adulthood. I've already told you I lost my mother to breast cancer when I was thirty-four. Five years later, my dad died of heart failure. Three months prior to that, my father-in-law died as well.

In 2005, my healthy, strong husband became sick. No one could figure out what was wrong with him until he almost slipped away and I brought him into Chicago. After undergoing a thoracotomy, he was diagnosed with sarcoidosis, an autoimmune disease that attacks the lungs. He went on to have several blood disorders that landed him with many pulmonary embolisms. In 2019, he had a heart attack and stroke on the same day due to blood clots. He now has a pacemaker and defibrillator implanted in him. He has been hospitalized more times than I can count since his sarcoid diagnosis for opportunistic infections and pneumonia. He has not worked since 2005.

In 2019, Matthew was twenty-nine and diagnosed with papillary thyroid carcinoma. He underwent a radical removal of his thyroid, surrounding tissue, and numerous lymph nodes, five positive for metastasis.

I tell you this so you realize where Matthew was coming from as he questioned God listening to us.

I have a different outlook on it. God loved his son so much that he allowed him to die on the cross for our sins. God gives these pauses in life because he has given us so much. He believes and trusts that we will show his undying love here on earth by ministering to others through our acceptance and growth through our difficulties.

The following is a journal entry after that night. I still pray that Matthew will understand that adversity promotes a closer relationship with God and how precious the opportunity is.

I haven't written in a while as I have been in a holding pattern between radiation treatments and Letrozole. Three days ago I took my first dose of Letrozole. This will block the production of estrogen and progesterone in my body for the next five years. Because my cancer is HR+ and Her2—it feeds off of these hormones to flourish and spread. I must say I'm not too enthusiastic about the immediate side effects, but time will tell, and perhaps they will diminish as days go on.

The other night Matthew came in and wanted to talk. He seems to be angry at the obstacles our family has faced. His Dad's illness, his cancer, my cancer have all weighed on his mind. I asked if he had talked to God about this, he replied God doesn't hear me, why should I bother? I told him it comes from deep within—a fragment of his soul, that is what must speak to God. Reassuring him that our pain must be had in order to grow and become closer to God. The very next day a friend posted a story on Facebook that seemed to sum it up better than my words to Matt ever could. It told of two children playing with glow sticks. The younger one was happy to just hold it and look at it, when the older child grabbed it from him, and bent it in half, releasing the color into the stick. At first the younger cried, when his brother said, "I had to break it so you could get the full effect." The story goes on to say, just like people. Some have perfect lives, they never have trouble, and are quite content. Others need to be broken and bent to realize their full effect in this world.

I am a hugely imperfect person. I have made many mistakes, hurt family and friends beyond measure. I have surrounded myself in a selfish cocoon and given little regard to those around me. I have wept at the foot of my parents graves, begging them to help me be the woman they dreamed I would be. But, I am human, and in the end, May my goodness outweigh my weakness. As I read this story above, what I always felt in my heart about the reason for my cancer, suddenly was put to words. As I navigate my brokenness, I will take refuge in the illuminating light that follows.

ReBirth

She had never seen the sun
Looking up, an unmet warmth filled her face.
Looking out, the sea met her with sapphire beams.
Her ignorance of beauty was not hers to own.
A lifetime of agony swept away on obstinate waves.
Moment by moment her anger became a distant stranger.
Her destiny fell into lost dreams
Her breath gave life to her soul.
Only then could she embrace the warmth of the sun,
Or freshness of the sea.
It was, by all means,
Her rebirth.

Teri Carlson

About the Author

Teri Carlson is a wife, mother of three, and grandmother of five. She is a recent breast cancer survivor, the inspiration behind this book. She has been married to her husband Doug for forty-one years and lives in the suburbs of Chicago.

She has written for years but never entertained the thought of being published—mainly authoring blogs, Facebook posts, and small editorials in local newspapers. Her hobbies are refurbishing antiques and collecting them. She has a small shop in co-op selling her furniture and antiques.

She also plays the guitar and has been in several church choirs. In her teens, she would play at local coffee shops and for weddings. Her real pride and joy comes from her grandchildren and watching them grow. She has been blessed with five of them, ages seven to seventeen: Riley, Cole, Chayse, Natalee, and Ella Grace.

CPSIA information can be obtained
at www.ICGtesting.com
Printed in the USA
BVHW090606161121
621700BV00016B/566